MW00944611

Opening the Doors

Poems by
Judith Adams

A ROBIN PRESS BOOK

"Let everything happen to you. Beauty and terror. Just keep going. No feeling is final"

– RILKE

Circling the Wagons

The things you got away with
at the back of the class,
smoking behind the gym,
all kinds of shenanigans.
Radical pilgrims hit the road with a
god that argues household religion.
To be an elder is to venture
further in all conditions.
This could be your last tube of toothpaste
or pair of blue jeans.
By all means have your
bags packed for the final journey
before circling the wagons of those we love.
It is pouring with rain
it's musical adagio, a relief.
The garden looking back with intensity.
I put my face down into the dirt
between flowers in case
heaven is frugal.
We circle the wagons in the
embers of our days.
On the minus side grasping,
on the plus love.
I must climb through rainbows,
turn my face to the tempest
where seabirds crack the sky.
And first thing in the morning
row out to partner the sunrise.
Every day closer to the
winds of the universe.

A place Inside

You have a place inside of you,
no-one can touch.
Overgrown with protest,
thorn, scorn and
gilded lily, the
household of suffering.
Do not work to rule,
walk out,
better the raging storm
that forces sore complaint.
Begin today, begin now
not made of God
angels or Gustav Mahler's
Symphony of a Thousand,
but deep down divinity of
your own footsteps
in the dark.

Autopsy on an Elephant
For David

Tonnage of bone, breathless
landscape of organs and mileage of hide.
The fall of a Buddha, fortress of the
African Bush, a massive silence.
I know how the elephant got his trunk,
kneeling beside Kipling's Limpopo.
Cushioned circumference of softly
sagging steps into the cracked
earth of a great continent.
What happens inside us when
something mighty falls; a moving
cathedral chorused over high grass,
curve of tusk, expanse of flank and
generous blanket of ears?
Were you given a knife and was
everything counted and weighed?
The twenty pound liver larger than a
piglet or a swan; the intestines,
junctions and twists that
conduct leaves, twigs and fruits.
The twin islands of kidneys filtering water
siphoned though the pendulum of trunk.
Was there an interested dentist to
extract the teeth, like pieces of mahjong?
When finally the heart was gently levered out,
did you want to fall on your knees and weep?

Apology

I have taken thongs, the red ones
lace and sequins, a hot
string between my cleavage.
A hidden exuberance that
enters the room in secret
sparkling with possibility,
like sunrise and sunset that
permeate the rim with potential.
The frilly little engine that motors me.
As my hair grays and
wrinkles assemble, people
talk about invisibility.
Ridiculous!
With this sparkling contraption
I give the finger,
straddle youth and dotage with
clandestine style.
Put on good music,
dim the lights,
dance with me,
read poetry,
talk philosophy,
be tender and
I guarantee
I'll go wild.

The Great Escape

Snow melted the morning.
The river rose, swelling the
breweries, restaurants and shops.
Its' energetic rush sweeping
dark kegs of beer, tossing
the yeast and hops through the town.
Hearing of the great escape,
loitering teenagers joined the revelry,
the gods in a loopy mood.
That is how the taxi driver,
as he drove us to the airport,
remembered that fantastic day;
barrels wrapped in blackberries
mud surfing the rocks, vagrant vittles
floundering until apprehended.
The townsfolk swigging heartily to the
plea of proprietors to return them
empty if they must.
Sometimes life breaks free.
Policemen smile, the homeless and underage
as much guest, as the rich and famous.

Capricious Muse

Put on your poetic black belt
and fight for an entrance.
Mention the hummingbird,
snow on the peaks, even what shocks
like Rilke's "God is growing."
or Sharon Olds' "My father came
into my sister's room like Hitler into Paris."
Gate crash.
Before you know it
you'll be hauling in the words.
Your rhetorical sails caught by
the gale force of expression.
One line a start, trash it,
squeeze it into the middle,
give it the honor of the last line,
or let it swerve into heartache and rescue.
Stake the poem down,
don't let it sag, whatever you do
don't abandon your sweet reader
in a swamp of confession.

Hooked in

Children pose before they know they exist.
At play in synthetic streets, prowling artificial
neighborhoods of shadowless blue lights.
Infidels from presence, drawn to digital lovemaking.
We leave our disheveled allotments starved of affection,
prostrating before iClouds that keep us from ourselves,
from walking the frozen pond, the woods and
summer fields, daisies rubbing knees in passing.
Sooner or later time moves into the red, we run low.
In dismay at absence, our practice
simulated, our devotion misplaced in
poignant redundancy.

Your Old Desk

You want to get rid of your desk.
It isn't as easy as that.

You sailed her through Sundays,
your creaking ship of launching thoughts,

outraged letters to officials,
speeches and liberal manifestos,

above juggernaut slant of the
London gutter, below.

Your cigar lit after a good lunch.
Aromatic thoughts weaving the

afternoon until the rain stopped.
We brought her across the Atlantic,

her compartments filled with the weight of
the family; old pictures of Oxford,

your father's fading ski maps,
birth certificates, as they came.

This is where your shoulders were the
broadest, where you would sit for

hours, house-hold affairs in analytical
overdrive, leaping up in delight to see me!

We must have a severing ritual for
casting-off to the Pacific Northwest,

from our old life, our younger years,
to shelter in a basket of trees,

the moon adrift in mist above
the eagle's nest, the mountains and sea.

First Year Anniversary of your Death

Darling , you would love to be
married to me now.
I am taking seriously tax forms
I used to mislay,
no longer nonchalant
about the bills, and have
labelled everything in the
cock-pit of the utility room.
The key to the safe is under the
Buddha with instructions.
In a nutshell I have grown up!
Sorry you had to take such
drastic steps on my behalf.
We always wanted for the
other what we wanted so
desperately for ourselves.
You insisted on security,
responsibility, duty,
enough funds for the grandchildren.
I wanted to speculate the intangible,
to sign up for the latest retreat.
Because of your industry,
I drummed up the next
pilgrimage, or couples workshop.
Now you know my thoughts

were not always loving;
choosing the best cup of tea
with the perfect amount of milk or
taking the cream off the yoghurt.
God forbid what else I
grabbed for myself.
Rilke said, God is growing,
a radical thought.
Why not our relationship?
You have more influence
where it really matters now.
Let's keep finding each other.
I saw you yesterday in the garden
drinking from the bird bath,
as if time was no longer an issue.
Don't pretend you can now keep silent.
I have heard the gods
are already complaining!
I miss your entrances
and exits and your
ecstatic homecomings.

I Miss

I miss bundling you into the car.
What it took to gather
our stuff, lunch, books, your
music and my small occupations.
I miss going through the kiosk
at the ferry and especially the
wind at the front of the boat,
even the lonely thoughts there.
I miss the express way,
the things we we would talk about,
the nice man in the car park
pressing the button for the first floor.
I miss seeing you emerge from your
blood draw, checking to see I had
your briefcase and hearing
how skilled she was.
I miss cruising on up to the fourth floor,
the soft chairs, the nobility in very sick faces,
and wondering when we would be called.
The weight check, I don't miss that, I came to dread it.
I miss waiting in that little room, the outside
world made into sections by a venetian blind.
I miss hoping the doctor would find
"the little guys" had shrunk.
That never happened.
We laughed when she said,
she only wanted the numbers,
she did not need your body

or your soul for that matter.
I miss getting you home and
tucking you in the Day Bed
with the dogs, and preparing dinner.
Most of all I miss the journey upstairs,
helping you navigate each step
which in the end became impossible,
and washing you like a child, the relief
on your face to be under the blankets,
all the exertion come to rest.
I miss kissing you goodnight
but I don't miss being
available for the moon,
lying beside you trying to imagine
what kind of death you would have
and whether I would be strong enough
to go with you, and how much pain you
might have. And I so miss you writing your book,
announcing to friends not to have restraint,
to just do it. And I miss the way you surrendered
your sadness about leaving us,
which is the hardest.
I miss all this because
I still had you.

Four percent
For Bruce

You sailed your desk
through our marriage,
paid bills, school fees,
and bailed the kids
out of dubious escapades.
As your moorings loosened from the
shores of your life, you sat up with
final proclamation:
"Four percent is four percent."
Still captain, still wanting to say from the
dark corridors of leaving:"I love you,
stay safe, don't exceed the
sustainable rate of withdrawal (in
fiduciary circles safe.)
Steer clear of the muddy waters of risk,
give deficit a wide berth.
Be British, frugal and sensible.
Four Percent is not capricious
but biblical in prophesy.
Live well, with a moral compass
and though I no longer
fill your sails in the
sparkling winds of our love,
I breathe extraordinary air behind you.
Darling, you are doing famously."

I have kept myself busy, though
the nights refuse my conquering pace.
No way to silence its' images,
no blinkers for its' hoarse demands.
Had I a wish from God Almighty,
one more dinner. It would be historic.
I would tell you my regrets,
we would laugh at memories.
You came out of the snow in your father's
world war coat, brief case,
distinct flat-footed walk, lost in thought.
My hand in your large, safe ones.
who cares about the pumpkin metamorphosis,
as long as everything had been said,
as long as our embrace is never again
torn apart over the gone furlongs of time.

Lights Out

Each night I turn the lights out,
and I go on and on talking to you,
who has left society, the planet,
the secular, the profane.
It is endless waiting for your text,
the echo of your large feet gone silent.
What were we thinking,
some benevolent angel
would lend you her cell phone?
I want to march across the border to find you
with a visa for your return, and
set the table for two.
Lets make a dash for it.
I want to know how you live,
how you exist in death.
Does love carry on or change
into a dazzling orb?
Does intimacy have the same
comforting embrace; a reality in your
world as it is in mine?
And darling, do you still love me
in the same extraordinary way?

Do Not Wait

Do not wait for a diagnosis to
change you by brute force.
The rafters of your ribs
beneath mud and snow,
buried in the final fields,
as the sun disappears.
Live as if a great war
had just ended,
The treaty; tolerance
compassion, and celebration.
Your official signature on the
complicated and demanding love
document worth more than anything.

Men of Art

Oh men of art beware!
Your masterpiece has a razor edge.
You choose your station as
if no one else shared your bed.
Muscular lovers, book writers, painters and
poets whose wooing defies the finest
mastery of scales, major and minor.
Look upon those who merely
live, who work the night shifts,
who aspire to nothing at all
but tenderness in the dead of night.
Oh men of art beware!
Bow down to the worn out cashier
who rings you up, her
pale face, a work of magnitude,
madonna of all madonnas,
adored by the gods.
Bow down, before it is to late,
defiled, lamenting on the ground
wishing to be nothing more
than the boy who hurls papers
at your door.

What People Say

For Kitty

That is the hard part, the world goes on.
Grief's raw premises, slow to vanish like an English winter.

People cross the road out of consternation,
or they say, "life is full of loss, put a limit on grief."

Or they ask, "is the house for sale?" and then relate,
years ago, uncle Jim died, how hard it was.

The truth is, the heart is authentic in loss, the ego
awkwardly shifts from foot to foot in a sacred environment.

You leave the harbor making for the depths of
heaving sadness. Little by little, alone, you adjust

your sails in the haunted winds, yourself as
friend, forged by the love you had.

Slowly, very slowly, you square into the night.
You feel a new breeze over the vibrant sunrise,

your arms flung wide, shouting, "Yes."

Giving Birth

Buffeted by the
tides of her womb's thrust,

she groans for the gods to
pay attention to the feminine force.

At last, the glistening head
crowns in the stretch of perineum and

draws on the dregs of her energy's
industrial, deep-throated moan.

In altered depths of primal magnitude,
a curled and bloodied entrance,

fetal fold of arms and legs.
She falls back on the pillow,

her face lit glorious, like of moon,
her breasts and thighs open to the world.

The umbilical cord glistening on her quivering
mound; all flesh, all soft.

In cry of wonder she demands to
hold him in all his revelation.

Their skin meets, the bond is done.
In the afternoon light,

his eyes search for the bell
of voice he once heard.

In the meadow of arrival,
a forlorn bleating, a fledgling protest,

incredulous speech
for the House of Commons.

Then, nudges for the nipple,
for the thick, health-giving colostrum.

His suck and latch informing the
pharmacist in the breast to adapt.

And the small milk-wheels get going
in the little factory of love.

The Heart That Belongs with Yours
(for the marriage of Tom and Emma)

Birds cover great distances in the
wind slip of current just as

you fly today in formation before the
great expanse of your lives.

A vow of love is a courageous utterance.
Its' fierce offices demand constancy and

confidence in declaration.
Again and again return to

where love is minted for the
robust imperative of destiny.

Look freshly at each other's face over the
Vegemite and offer each day to do

one thing to make life easier and
thank profusely.

Take the heart that belongs with yours and
give a wide berth to each other's freedom.

Lean in against the gale force of your
beloved's becoming, and your own.

In the trade winds of tandem love, you
create more beauty than is possible by yourselves.

First Born

Last night a small knock at the door.
My daughter came dressed for bed,
carrying her first born, swaddled in
geometric perfection.
So I could see his face,
she leaned him like a little log towards me,
his eyes, half-focused pools of glimmering light.
If I was in the habit of reeling off a
hundred powerful prayers,
they would not come
close to this parcel of divinity.

Watching my Daughter's Baby

It is double-duty,
he come to no harm.
This miracle from my womb's
second womb.
Under the bamboo
where doves call,
geraniums, raspberries and the
wheelbarrow drifting
in and out of his pram,
and his dreams.

Dropping in for Breakfast

Early into the city,
I swing to my daughter's house.
She might be flustered before work;
the breast pump, pureed vegetables,
emergency phone numbers,
house key, teats and her own buttery milk.
The sun comes with me through the door.
There she is, her baby at her heels.
He gathers up his little knees into
alternate rhythm; plonk, plonk, plonk plonk,
knee, hand, knee, hand, like a well-oiled egg
heading towards my legs.
These moments cannot be applied for
or made from deals under the table.
They come out of the blue like the
old fashioned puzzle you shake,
hoping the silver balls fall
perfectly into the dips.
In daily terms, perfection.
You pocket it,
like a love letter.

So Long

So long as there is divide,
black, white, and all the in-betweens.
So long as wherever you go,
you make assessment,
though your comforts feel solid,
they have no lasting ease.
Your eyes are mine,
leaf, mushroom, blade of grass,
spider's breath and apple,
red cheeked upon your own.
Some want to save the planet
from it's tilt towards annihilation.
Some grasp at all they can
for the pleasure of a blink of time.
Others hate the difference they find and
children grow shallow confidence by appearance.
Our judgements a gavel,
hard down on every surface.
Rest in the duende of it all;
stars assembling indigo night,
your slow walk to the oak's limbs
also, in your arms and legs.
How then can you be of one religion,
one color, one thought, one entity?
The bare branch outside your door is calling you
to death, as much as spring calls to life;
to love the scarlet poppy as
the crow's delinquent strut.
Each cell a creation in the
swagger of life's arrant mystery.

Blessing for Wesley Robin - August 2016

One star in the indigo night
carried you to the parents you have chosen.
The sheltering trees, hear the distant
sound of the sea coming in under the moon.
Walk on the crystal frost of winter and
listen for the voice of the wind that carries your future.
Never loose sight of the reason you are here.
Take care of this gently turning planet.
Pay attention to your yearning, awaken to what is invisible.
Do not be afraid to announce who you are.
The levity of your smile is your heart's currency.
Give your guardian angel free range.
Trust her whims and imagination, she will never leave you.
Question everything and come to your own philosophy.
Let your days be measured by dignity.
Remember, there are those you cannot see who
want to help you within the deep embrace of
your belonging.
Dear Wessy,
we bless your waking,
your sleeping, your ups and downs
your encounters, your loves and the
mysterious promise of your life.
In the fertile shade of your heart,
on this day we plant our blessing.

Jack and His Wild Flowers

He was only three.
From his window wild flowers
charmed the earth.
Monet could not have done it better
but for no poppies.
Texas has a softer side, we all do;
Blue Bonnets, yellow daisies,
and the doves daylong call.
For the sake of his sister's
birthday the weeds and colorful
companions needed mowing;
Jack's glorious kingdom,
on death row in the sun.
After all, he had not seen
any other world, this was his miracle to be
destroyed for barelegged girl's s'mores and Piñata.
Until the last minute the scattered
palette adorned his dreams.
Terrible things happen to a boy's heart.
The mower cut, like a barber to
golden curls, snipping petals and blooms.
Jack cried out from his bedroom,
"No, daddy, no, daddy, no!"
What could a man do, straddled
between his daughter's sparkle for a party
and his little boy's broken heart?
Keep shouting, Jack.
Keep protesting for beauty.
And Jack …never give up.

Oranges and Lemons

I hated birthday parties.
Battlefield of taffeta
balloons, streamers,
chocolate fingers, sandwiches,
jelly, sausages and sweet cake that
sliced your head.

The break free;
bossy girls with curls
in whispering clutches,
dreaded games looming;
Musical Chairs, Grandmother's Footsteps,
as cut-throat as Parliament.

Pass the Parcel to practice grasping,
Chinese Whispers to practice gossip.
Simon Says.. touch your nose,
you touch your knee and
a boy points in ridicule,
(the one never to marry.)

"Oranges and Lemons says the bells of St Clements"
To be the last with a "candle to light
you to bed" alone between the
arms of taller girls -
"Here comes a chopper to
chop off your head."

My Old Mother

She stood in the doorway,
a frail welcome wagon,
a single autumn leaf
clinging to a multitude of loss.
The kettle on,
biscuits, like repeated stories,
in the same battered tin.
How long was I staying,
would I always live in America?
She flipped through the
newspaper and fixed on an ad,
as if it were the editorial;
sipped her whisky, then
announced it was
high time for a drink!
The moon hung in the courtyard.
She shut the doors,
jabbing with the wrong key;
perplexed and irritated and
clinging to the banisters,
as if a strong wind was
delaying her voyage in the last,
fierce currents of her life.
We have mostly locked horns,
my own self in her struggles,
her categoric conclusions,
her emphatic declarations.

In my panic to find the exit,
a high speed train home,
I am plagued by sadness,
and my own heartlessness.
She appeared at the
top of the stairs,
without her teeth,
her face collapsed and tiny;
a gnarled bark of tree
peering down at me,
an old mountain woman.
I loved her more than anything
in that moment.
She was pure beauty,
pure spirit, so illuminated,
she was terrifying.

In Praise of Bases

I write from the alto section,
though I am of a high register
I prefer a saner existence.

We all have one memory of the
inevitable woman clinging
on cold Sunday mornings to the

last note, as if to let it go, she might
lose her own species.
Although I admit, when the

angels really come, I get
goose bumps, like when a
mother is really a mother and for that

she takes full responsibility.
Tenors, those musical
saints, make harmony so others

can exist in beauty. And then
I am brought to tears.
The basses, yielding to vibration,

the deep rumbling of the real
father, returning to the
melody lost in the womb, lost

for the erotic thrust of the world.
Women, look at the faces of
your sons, the gentleness of

his hands doing daily things.
Remember the love scene,
how he washed her hair,

his sonorous voice
tenderly preparing her
for love.

The Barn

I must have been eight,
strong enough to open
the barn door next to
the milking herd,
noses down into fields of hay.
It was the beginning of Autumn.
The floor swept, dust collecting
in places outside of the broom.
I could smell the spade, the rake,
the pitch fork and overalls
hanging by one strap.
Straw piled to the rafters and
swallows noisily preparing
their wind journey south.
Scanning the dark shadows,
I looked up to a small window,
partly covered by derelict
cobwebs, in diffuse light.
Unblinking, a white barn owl
stared into me,
into who I was at eight.
It turned its' head,
then slowly back.
I couldn't move
before such scrutiny.
Shaken, I backed out,
for the first time knowing
my own name and
why I had been born.

Joining Texas Task Force
For William

Dangling over rapids,
roped to a Black Hawk helicopter,
you descend into a hero's journey.
Death is getting the upper hand,
flood taking everything in sight.
You lower to a car suspended on a stump.
Strapped together, swing and spiral to
reach the side door under the whirling blades.
You always responded to crisis,
everything magnified and meaningful.
You save lives because you know what to do,
you know how to have eye contact
with a person thrashing around for air.
Tomorrow you will be high in the
mountains searching for a fallen pilot.
How easily we are lost, how lucky to be found.
Things happen, though we live
oblivious to the wild edge.

The Bodhisattva
For Rick

To find the Sicilian,
look for a polished pate,
with mahogany shine,
distinctive glow above
tropical vibrance of
astonishing shirts.
Look for the man striding
through town with two
fluffy white and disgracefully
indulged appendiges.
Go towards the music.
It flows out of him like an
Irishman's stories from the bones.
A musical life sings and goes with the flow.
When real distress happens,
a philosophical mechanic,
a first responder, a heart cathedral
that takes in sorrow.
We all care selectively
but this man universally,
not confined only to domestic loves,
but all on this spinning planet.
The man's wife is no pushover,
in resignation, and sometimes
disbelief, he smiles indulgently
basking in her risk-taking;
as one more announcement
stuns the breakfast table.

And on a walk in the woods,
stares into space as she
fumbles beneath her skirt to establish
mileage attached to her knickers.
After all, marriage demands flexibility.
We all want to help, but few of us
get on the train for distant strife.
This is a man who pulls people out of
past images, fires up the lights and the music,
and at the peak of festivities
sets off for the house in disarray,
unobtrusive in magnitude of suffering.
When summer comes he leaves for the
island of slow ferries and gathers together
those who make a difference.
Under the naked moon
with naked friends in a hot tub
conversations begin that incubate and
blossom for a world, hard down on the
accelerator, in great need of a maverick
who insists we wake up.
He is the foot soldier, the
night watchman, the lover,
the carer, the player of Jazz,
the listener, the advocate,
the untethered bodhisattva
who crosses continents
for the sake of the heart.

For Gloria's Leaving

You are leaving the village
that has brought you up.

Liberal thinking, touchy feely
practices that have shaped you.

Who knows what town square you will arrive at,
what philosophy you might level out in.

Take your violin with you in case you need it.
It brings us to our knees, but the

girl who plays it, is the one we love; that look,
that certain slant of light, maturity of soul and grace.

It is the shoes that end the portrait,
they have sparkled at every size,

and today walk you with discriminating alacrity.
We are the elders and have no advice.

The motor of your life is under full throttle,
make sure your yearning belongs to you,

not the village nor your parents.
Fly solo with your thinking.

Don't squander your star. Let it travel into
back streets, palaces and slums; where the

only instrument is a dustbin lid.
God is not interested in which class you take,

or whether you practice ten hours a day. She wants
you to offer yourself to the world in the shape of yourself.

You have choices the mass-man does not have,
and artistry that changes lives.

But remember, the piazza and the village green
are for kissing. Make sure you are good at it.

The Actor Accepts The Part

To act is to be someone
you don't know.

How else do you break
habits locked inside?

How else do you let go of
your own restrictions,

corners and edges;
your carefully built belonging,

as you fumble for the line
in electrifying silence?

Have you ever seen the Pope dress?
An elaborate affair so he

moves with grace that
qualifies his customized wave.

Put on a costume and find the
spotlight where you get a

break from yourself;
detective, butler, swooning virgin or cad.

I knew a little girl who was
a cucumber frame in her first role,

impressive prerequisite for a
shakespearean soliloquy.

If you never play the miser,
the threadbare codger,

the princess, the hysterical son,
you will feel nothing in your bones

of the inner world of men and women
in shadow and light.

Gestation

Your heart must dwell in its own bundle.
Too soon exposed will be still born;
easy to crush what is fragile,
to shine a neon light on its' sacred universe.
A robin's egg shattered
under ferns and huckleberries,
from a branch she hangs her head.
Sorrow and happiness needs to incubate,
cradled in silence, safe from the
world's boxed inquisitions,
until ripe enough to hatch as
it's own mystery.

To Woo a Poem

No need for sharpened pencils or a quiet house.
If your body is ripe cancel your your dentist.
Listen for words in a mood for jazz.
If you fear the poem's power
I know what that's like,
Let words present themselves,
especially those with rhythmic
tandem ability, prone to truth.
If a swan appears instead of snow
consider it lucky.
Prepare to undress in front of your critic.
Warning: If a verse happens to set off
under its' own steam,
don't dilly-dally, let it cause
goosebumps in the back of your neck
as you bail out superfluous pronouns.
The poem's motor must hum and its'
title must have status.
If you become self-conscious,
metaphors rebel childishly,
so find something else
in the house that needs doing.

Love by Writing the Title

My eldest confided
"I do not know, if I can love"
I think I told her it takes a lifetime,
or perhaps I missed the chance
to tell her to take loving gently.
Tend it like a homestead.
All weather and seasons
must be the same to it.
Get your foot in the door, write the title.
It has unseen prospects, the rest will follow.
But more than likely, you,
my dear girl, are a natural-born lover.

First Lipstick

It was Lacome "Bois de Rose",
my first lipstick.
That luxurious smell of my
new, sixteen year old self.
Uncharacteristically, my mother
bought an expensive make.
She thought, perhaps,
it would represent my future
marriage to some well-launched,
well-breeched dude.
Instead, I went to America
with a man who looked like
Che Guevara, a liberal renegade.
I still wear the lipstick,
proof of my own possibilities,
my own way to kiss,
my own way to kneel before
my own wonderful life.

What Can I Say

Inadequate to speak to you of your journey,
though I want to take your hand.
I don't know how.

Our leaving exhausts all forms of
dissolution and still,
miracles always possible.

I want to share with you this,
I don't know what to make of it.

In a dream my beloved said,
"Come with me, it is easy.
Fall forward, let yourself go,
drop down into the vortex"

Though you are holding your breath,
in the release you begin to
float among a million stars.
You have never experienced love like this.

In a another dream, he lay
under oriental blankets. Again he said,
"It is easy, let go."

Then he changed slowly to a
wizened old man, and in that moment
curled in embryo preparing for the
thrusting tunnel of birth.

In the blink of an eye we follow each other.
We tumble towards the hand we have
held and the heart that has dwelled in ours.

Charlie's Death

Sometimes death comes between birdsong;
sparrow, robin, the call of doves.
One eagle in the know flies to a close by
tree and a leaf falls.
High in the mountains a village
gives milk to it's babies, as the
moon drifts in her phases
above mountain peaks.
How will the city look?
Will vendors close up shop
and Apostles flee the cathedrals?
For Charlie there was a wind.
The apple tree full of movement,
red globes bouncing around
like the gifts you have spread wide,
your own harvest waving at your window.
The house full of loved ones and beloved songs.
We are learning how to deliver dear ones to the ferryman.
There are people standing by, waving, giving last hugs
and whispers, not knowing what adventures await.
Fires burn low in Africa, sunset aglow with potency.
If you stand by the ocean as winter approaches
you will get an inkling of the majesty of
what awaits all of us.
Who can predict the season?
Christmas lit with lights, high summer when

poplars converse with the warm night or
when snowdrops have bartered with darkness.
The moment of dying is not random.
All the forces of our birth arrive to help.
A great spirit calls forth celestial workers
for they have been told that this is a special one.
Flags and flowers adorn the path down to where your
moorings are loosened by invisible, holy hands.
If we allow ourselves God's imagination
we will fall to our knees before death's nobility.
This man straddled the planet with capacity for love,
to foster others to find their own pilgrimage,
not out self-importance but a consecrated need to help.
A tall Angel, who entered the room with mischief,
to stir up the status quo and get people dancing.
Not an ordinary foxtrot, but ecstatic and wild,
particularly the young for their genius.
Not for a minute did Charlie squander any of it,
any of his own fiercely passionate life.
I want that for myself. Do you too?

XTC

Fearing it, wanting it's breakthrough
from the heart's fortified anthem,
exploding inwards, unraveling from moorings,
from life's bundle to a mythical cocoon.
Rock and moan to the core, to gather up losses.
Taking the hands of friends, soft and pearl-like.
She lists her love's sweet refrain.
Bach, in exact emotion, flings
fireworks into the heart and holds the clouds in space.
The eyes of a friend, as if a megalith had pupils,
prepared to stay unknown distances.
Time leaves the premises.
The father's repeated invasions
of what is sacrosanct; demon, man,
half-man, destroyed-man,
made whole by fragility.
In love, go through.
Bushwhack for the spot and
hold hands with the best and
worst of angels.

Ahmed of Aleppo

Born into bedlam and boy time,
your scrawny chest entrapped,
barely beating out of the rubble,
set concrete around you.

The cries, the drill cutting into
the casket of rock at your waist.
Men shouting, "Don't sleep Ahmed
keep reciting, you can do it, don't sleep!"

They broke you free.
Your siblings and parents crushed
beneath lacerated walls.
Ahmed we have seen you.

We have seen your blood stained face.
We know your playmates have gone.
We hold you here, right here, in our hearts.
Rise up against hate.

Rise up for love.
We cannot ask you to forgive.
Who are we, who live in comfort,
to say anything?

Bernie and the Bird

Bernie stopped his speech about the
need for equal pay and healthcare.
A diminutive green bird had
arrived on the campaign stage.
To the surprise of political decorum,
it went further and landed on the
podium next to his right hand.
A tiny heart oblivious of significance.
The crowd went wild and that's the thing,
the proceedings came to a halt
in ecstatic excitement.
A humble happiness as if to say
by the tilt of his head,
there is more to life than what you
are saying; wind, clouds
collecting over mountain tops,
rivers, sparkling summer dawns,
and between branches the
music of leaves falling
at the end of summer.
Surely rapture and wild energy
restores faith in the original heart.
Bernie stood still and smiled
to the roar of appreciation,

especially from the young,
merely for the love of significance.
There is symbolism in it's little
wings of freedom, it was really a dove
proclaiming peace and
No More War.
Its' uncluttered livelihood
proof there is another way.

Flamenco Protest at the Bank

We flounder in fiscal uncertainty,
clinging to our own decline.
You stiffen your posture, refusing indignity.
You do not deflate nor crumple,
but move as though the city
had not shut its purse.
Every step, every stamp of revolt
poised in dignity and defiance of low-paid
rejections, power you across the floor.
Your chin, raised above the world
as air flares your nostrils, protests
everything but equal dominion.
In the course-throated lament's outcry,
you lift your layered skirts of freedom,
and flaunt dissent in the face of regulation.

Night Journey

Terrified by death
for the world finishes there.
I have read everything;
still, no great revelation.
So I climb onto the back of a bird,
a cuckoo if you like, to distant lands.
Feeling its downy feathers,
I lie long between beating wings,
journeying north, surrendering
to the chill in the air, as I ascend
to the glimmer of stars
in the deep indigo night.
You would not believe how close
the breath-taking curve of the moon.

Lullaby for the World

In the hush of the gods,
who will rock the world
in her cradle of grief?
Blood spilling out in worsening
brutality is the new ordinary.
Fleeing families clamber on deflating death boats.
The moon with lessening hope,
stares down in disbelief.
The planet, torn from her seasons,
is gathering fire, wind and tidal confusion.
Call in the healers to restore traumatized hearts.
especially terrified children.
And, like the first crocus in the bleakest cold,
begin to stir in unfathomable darkness towards light.

.

Run By Nuns

For Bennett

Man… you want a
three week silent retreat.

Hard to imagine you can
do without the feminine.

A monastery up in the quiet hills
and you walking along the

path to the copper-colored mountain.
Monks nod, knowing the territory.

You want to eat simply,
to live simply, have

conversation with the divine.
Undiluted, filling the heart

that is already big.
What is the latest?

Great, you have found a retreat,
small and pastoral, and

Oh yes,
run by NUNS!

So my Call to you is This
Dedicated to PT

Let poems blossom in your hands.
Among the petals, you regain
composure for work.
Arrive to a host of golden daffodils
where the heart speaks openly.
Words shift in the lilt of each other
to comfort, scold and harass you for a larger life.
Open all your windows for whatever
blows in, and let the stuck
door on its' creaking hinges
usher vagrant metaphors.
Words come trouping in to
speak of what you never knew you knew.
The genius of imagination
finds language for all its' people.
A rhyming voice
makes the child a mystic.
How we abandon agenda, how we
choose our lines, is the power of one.
Be the the nurse log
that lets sprout even the
dark tread of what you fear.
It is the footfall of angels,
light -hearted and profound in
our cherished humanity.

Late Developer

I used to want to be taller,
have more curves,
and voluptuous hair.
Men would stop in
mid-sentence,
women also, as I
glided down the street
in bootleg jeans,
as visible as the cathedral spire
in summer, and as sexy.
With presentable looks,
I could have been party-minded
but stayed in my room
longing for something
I could not name.
So I played a musical
instrument badly
because of the
elegance it stood for.
Then one day,
there was a
marvelous explosion.

Thought

Gold-leafed pages do you no good when it comes to answering the Jackpot question -

What are you doing with your life?

Times for Flying Solo

You have said yes,
sometimes wanting to say no.

It's ok to live the way you do,
irritating to people who have schedules,

use hair spray, and whine a lot.
Climb onto a train to Manchester

with soccer hooligans, or hike without map,
refusing shrinkage to a fearful forecast.

If a pedicure is not wild enough,
things happen anyway, risk or no risk.

Beyond the garden
there's a party in full swing.

Invited, but comfortable on the patio,
double-dipped in good silence.

You contemplate sacred solitude,
a glass of wine by your side,

thoughts hushed by the drum's
distant gospel where they are dancing,

while you hang out in fugitive reflection
that blossoms in the dark.

Turn Around

This all started when a blogger noted how
he hovered over her in the second debate,
the disease still publicly infiltrating,
still a menacing presence.
Millions of women responded with their
own viral outrage.

In the pie-making kitchen a late and
harried employee, pink mini and white boots
triumphant to the pastry, the berries,
the large barrel of Crisco,
"It's a good day! I have a new phone
And my husband has gone back to prison."

Her voice a resonant bell sounding over the
village, declaring liberation.

I want to line up in a open field of poppies,
all women as far back as centuries allow
I would ask the wind to blow in their hair,
have them stand with their legs apart,
in warrior pose.
Opposite them, on their knees,

all men that have ever abused.
Have them weep for their savagery;
for their children beneath tables, crouched
behind doors, unprotected, in domestic isolation.
To feel the searing pain of brutality to the
womb that held in safety, each one of them.

Let the tender-hearted men nurture the bullies,
surround them in beauty, cure them of their father's
drunken entrances and destitute exits.

There is a groundswell that is gathering
despite politics, despite regression,
out of a desperate and long silence.
My sisters, my women, my sweet
young boys stay awake
for the whole truth.

I refuse to let this be the age of the tyrant
or sleep in the demolition of our making.
Turn around, turn around in your own small
workshop and pull out the hard wires,
the unforgiving coarseness, and yield to your
true nature, and never again starve it of affection.

What Binds You

Have you ever felt desperate,
in the heat of noon to find a wall to
lean on, as you dissolve into the
broken-down moment believing
your mind's ferocious accusations?
Have you ever felt death speeding towards you,
vows evaporating, blotching the
pathos of self-pity's whore?
And have you, after a time, walked home
deep in a maze of pain,
kidnapped by your modus operandi?
The dreaded approach, a room full of people,
smiling up at you from the kitchen table
conversation erratic and intelligent.
Your tears on the edge of rising like
city drains on the point of swell.
A scrap of diverted rubbish in unpredictable squalls,
you join the capricious winds of opinion.
Pulled along by the tenor of their voices
to a safer edge, it's possible to
recover enough to say what you need,
what you love, because your
personal affair no longer binds you.
So you tell the truth, all of it.
One after the other,
not caring if you never recover,
refusing to bed the old protocol.

When it is Said

The true mother tongue
cannot be learnt;
the rising moon,
a flock of white snowdrops,
birds jostling the apple tree.
Experience loses it's life when spoken.
Language forms at a sacred source.
What has already
been said is counterfeit;
someone else's small change
jingling in your pocket.
In the beginning was the word,
the logos, the silent language
of the universe, the
unspoken onomatopoeia.
And today on the news, a live recording
from the Rosetta Mission,
listen, the comet actually sings!

Christmas Birth

From the dark throb of birth
we are born to find a new articulation.
An expanding language that demands travel,
and courage to arrive free from
yesterday's conclusions, to walk into
Galilee or your local town for an answer to the
strange fact that we are born at all.
The simplicity of a stable is enough story.
Shepherds trip and slid in the dawn
from the cold hills, hats in hand on
unsure knees of reasoning.
The three wise men kneel also
in their royal jewels of intellect,
out of the desert's freezing night.
No legend is stagnant, if there
are pages to turn,
chapters to cross, tears to shed
and bewilderment to live through.
If you do not land in the first clearing,
you will in the third or fourth.
Eventually we find a space
in the world of things.
The occult moment when your
heart leaps and you dance with your
wayward god into the Christmas night.

Where we Exist

If you have stood at the entrance,
your heart hastening with awe
for the birth you are about to see,
then you know the true approach.

If you have been cradled in the
fork of a bough, gently
emerging into yourself,
then you have language.

If you have found a smile in the deficit
of a difficult morning, or clenched
encounter opening to understanding,
then you know the truth of possibility.

Snow upon snow, in the holy nights
chimneys articulate an assembly of
inner dwelling, clustered in a
frozen landscape, you sleep

with the bright petals of the moon,
the mother tincture,
the dream of gods–
where we exist.

True Elders

For Jim and Jo

Every village needs a pair of angels,
one with a tool belt that hammers out help,
and one with inclusive humor
that turns the world hopeful.
If you cruise the neighborhood,
keep your eyes on rooftops,
serious shoveling is flaunting
Medicare's protocol.
Jim, a first-responder,
sniffs out need with a
problem-solving motor.
He patrols the neighborhood
for stubborn drains,
electric seizures, anything
vaguely delinquent,
a calamity to put right.
But if there is a new car in the driveway,
that stops him dead in his tracks.
Upside down admiring the undercarriage,
the glamorous fender,
itching for a spin and final verdict.
His distinct, slightly-forward walk,
well-known calligraphy from
kitchen windows, followed by a little
appendage, considered by local canines
the sexiest in town.

Jim belongs to a notorious men's group,
don't ask what goes on there
unless you have a strong constitution.
Let me tell you about his partner in crime.
I would say, "Don't fuck with the Madonna!
She has a vision beyond yours,
she sums up the village and in a
split-second, knows who you are,
how to get the party going,
and the bashful to dress up in
something outrageous.
She has seen it all,
unshakable and unshockable.
As the body's bolts and screws loosen,
their determination made more
complete by attendance to what matters.
If there is a board to sit on,
they sit for as long as it takes.
This iconic couple show up
with quantum ideas to make the village thrive.
They are builders, connectors, and
wherever they go, bring favorable winds.
Their love is of industrial strength.
Tonight we celebrate what belongs to us.
Our angels. Our beloved Jo and Jim

My Editor
for Marilyn

A true friend is prepared to
argue whether colons and commas
should be scattered at random,
or if a line break is a good precipice.
Readers, are unaware what
happens in the kitchen
over many mornings with the
spices and sharp knives.
You showed up day after day to
wrestle with my words.
Your long finger nails making elegant
landings on 'A' 'G' or 'option'.
If you laughed and turned the page,
it was good but hesitation
merely because a sentence had
no verb, annoying.
Who would want to be
'coming' anyway midmorning
as colons assemble like uptight
poppers on a sexy dress.
You saved me from published illiteracy
This is just a thank you.
It is an achievement to be
Valedictorian, quite another
to be the heart's Cum Laude.

Healing Circles

A day can vanish
from the brightest beauty;
Shredded by a Physician's report
a putrid march through the one
who spins on a dark dime and
somersaults to where angels
tear apart in unsparing lyrics
and lamentation your lifestyle.
Isolation is not possible,
it never was true anyway.
So we band together,
we mind the light,
we form a circle around
the one being hauled away,
rehearsing in our own minds
what will also be ours,
the direction the same.
And there our knowledge ends.
We have theories, even small intimations.
We don't attempt to throw a life line,
but together construct a raft.
We climb in for the
ups and downs of the odyssey.
With aching, imperfect and
shattered hearts,
we close in on the mystery.

Opening the Doors for Each Other

Imposing circular entrances, your heart
beating to join the movement that
draws you in and drops you off -
the small explosion of arrival.
You are lost.
She puts her shopping down,
gestures a good way to go
marked by churches, roundabouts
and a hawthorne hedge.
We used to visit Mrs. Godling at the grocer.
Every item discussed; figs, salami,
sugar rations and daughters.
We crossed the road to borrow a lemon.
Now, the doctor backs out of the room
clutching his computer as you try to
explain your symptoms.
School workbooks counter imagination
into coffins of curiosity.
Attached to the wall, you once listened to your
father's lament, and gave solace.
The point is, if we can no longer
open the door for each other,
we no longer see the
upturned wheelbarrow alone
in the snow, as the train rushes past.

To Build a Nation

Birds chat and chirp in the rafters of the
ferry terminal from a large pipe fixed with spikes,
intended to block feathered construction.

Suspended between lethal skewers,
swallows refuse foreclosure with song.
Their ingenious fulcrum,

like a crooked row house in Amsterdam.
I thought then about the world,
how some want to fence people out.

Nature allows nature to squat where she will.
Nurse logs give birth to ferns and trees.
Owl knows which branch to wait upon the squirrels

and through dead leaves, mushrooms pummel into
diaphanous birth, sea shells drift back and forth
sliding beneath tides.

Using all comforts to be found,
we can make a tolerant and inclusive
dwelling for the assortment we are.

And with beating of drums insist
avarice falls to its' knees
one by one.

Then One Day

He sits in his highchair holding crumbled toast,
bits thrown over the bow.
Mom dances flamenco.
She does this most days;
unrestrained, her posture arched,
lifted and swooping like an eagle
or queen of queens.
Her hips measure the
world's capacity for the
power of the feminine,
palms pivot and interchange
in precise art of textured articulation.
She defies gravity with imagined
guitar and sonorous lament.
Her baby's spoon aloft, as he moves
in the womb of her dance, eyes glistening.
One day - it was this morning, and I was there -
he clicked his fingers and thumbs,
Olay! And we applauded his
ecstatic collaboration.

Calling the Lama

I am calling distant realms,
with my unsatisfactory prayers.
Still, Lama, I am calling, I am calling.
Send in your henchmen with handcuffs,
force me to the ground.
Pummel my heart into compliance.
There is no other way.
I can only fake it right now and
call out with little hope of
getting the top man, or anyone.
There must be an opening somewhere
for my weak devotion.
Oh Lama, can you hear me from so
far away when you already have
good people to see?
If one small plea could reach your ear
and for some strange reason you decide to reply,
ah then, my heart leaps!

To Be Touched

I saw God, or whatever name you give her,
in the high street.

She was tall,
I would not expect a tiny god.

Miserable,
I happened to walk to town

in the scruffy area of my emotions;
much to clean up, much to put right.

In that gloomy territory
she smiled. I liked her scarf.

Her face a fleeting compassion
as we passed the butchers,

the post office,
people walking the daily hour;

faces bouncing off faces.
Nobility and tenderness

etched in her eyes, a sweet
remedy working its' healing way,

as momentary as it was,
into the wounded place of my heart.

Buddha's Bowl

Went up stream against the current.
Proof of enlightenment bobbing happily.
The rest of the world frantic;
multiple footsteps rushing in the rain,
scuttling high heels, the city
caught in fascination for itself.
Over the landscape the sweet sigh of
impermanence enlivened by the morning's wind.
Beneath the moon swans float in
windswept white weddings,
frost all the way down Cathedral Hill and moorhens
along the banks close to snowdrops and ice melt.
Half wanting not to own anything and
definitely to be at least kind, more
generous than I have been to date.
Let me be the buddha's bowl
making my way in the
morning's imagination.

Standing Rock

Do not sit,
or lie down.
Stand in warrior pose.
The planet buckles to its' knees
wound upon wound.
Those who fill their bellies,
with toxins of avarice
do not deserve an apple,
a glass of milk,
the meat they devour,
worth only plastic from the
stomach of the dying albatross.
Those who care, mingling together,
in the cold of protest, supplies cut off
by politician's indifference.
Gather then with the birds,
compass of the winds,
rising and setting sun,
plains and mountains,
and tread lightly in falling snow
on this inviolable earth.
The young of the world
demand uncontaminated inheritance;
a passing on of the seed, the
bounty of allotment, serenity of
hills and the sweet music of bees.

They want an earth to cross,
diverse continents,
to lift those who suffer,
with remedies of encouragement
and sustaining days to partner
old age that belongs to us all.
A slowing heart beat
ebbing to the sound of
impartial prayers.

Sophia's Wisdom

If you are raped, say nothing,
do not go to the police.

I watched my mother's lips
say this to her daughters,

knowing what happened when
my father launched into her room.

My sweet women, we can reverse the
world's slippage.

Bring out what has been curtained by centuries,
your essays, your plans, your masterpiece

your flamboyant dresses, deciphering intuition, visions,
endurance and birth cries,

your genius and the genius of your daughters.
Muffle nothing.

In spectacular revolt,
heaven's virgins have bailed out to

.

love men for their soft side, their capacity for
adoration, but will never submit.

Help young men adjust to understand how you walk,
how you figure things out for global stability.

The Statue of Liberty is a woman who asks for the
huddled masses, inscribed in the approach.

Rank upon rank of sisters are with you.
The moon is looking down,

through a starless mist in a
universe daring to ponder salvation.

The Case for a Woman

The world has lost it's fulcrum.
Appetites climb, the homeless lurch from
one concrete bed to the next and
couples to a logistic kiss
before the graveyard shift.
What choice do we have but to take
the planet's plight seriously?
If we can't care for those,
without help, without medicine
and those running for their lives
then we are less than human.
It is women who resist violence,
women want to talk it over,
to connect and listen.
She has survived decades in the
government trenches as a foot soldier.
She has never left her post,
her eyes on a kinder horizon.
What is the alternative?
We all know the place of shadow
but a national decent, a catastrophe.
Bernie and the bird her talisman.
The young have a right to hope,
to sound a clarion call for the
earth to be tended and war ended,
each person valued for their stoic lives.
Let us tear down what separates,

with the bricks and mortar build homes,
schools and refuge for those fleeing monstrosity.
Capitalism does not work if its foundation is lust.
If we are happy while brothers and sisters
suffer, nothing will go well.
She stands for equality.
She knows the wreckage of bullies and
not afraid of pushback, to stand for what is right.
We do not have to be the all powerful thug
but a people that give to others in poor shape,
and establishes trust; a democracy that works for all.
What is the Declaration of Independence
if not a healthy premise from which to grow.
and grow we must.
Choose wisely, not from inflated
economic thirst but from a sane heart.

A place Inside

You have a place inside of you,
no-one can touch.
Overgrown with protest
thorn and scorn and
gilded lily, the
household of suffering.
Do not work to rule,
walk out,
better the raging storm
that forces sore complaint.
Begin today, begin now
not made of God
or angels
or Gustav Mahler's
symphony of a thousand,
but deep down divinity of
your own footsteps
in the dark.

Lullaby for my Father

You take yourself to bed in the paralyzed rubble
of violence for the walls to be struck
in a stupor of inebriated ascent,
holding your breath for the turn and slam
to prowling silence of a predator's den,
you finally fall to slumber.
Even now you wait for the violation of
unbridled unhappiness, as if a monster
clock was chiming through the years
at the late hour of his home coming.
Terror of the night's territory
though everything is safe.
Bring him down from unknown realms,
pain is working its' way through his heart.
Beckon him to your bedside, pull him towards you,
rock him to sleep with a lullaby.
You are almost seventy and his child,
though once you wanted him dead,
you are capable of understanding.
Take his trembling nicotine hands in yours.
Dance him around the room, through his Aspergers
his religious childhood, his shattered marriage,
his incapacity to tenderly love make and
sing St. Matthews Passion from beginning to end.
Build together a pilgrim's shrine,
the kind they have in the mountains,
with a madonna and plastic flowers,
a small sanctuary that welcomes the darkness,
the moon and stars, the soft even breath of sleep.

Hiroshima
BBC documentary

On the brick stairs in the center of the city,
a shadow of a man vaporized on the spot.

Candles float down the river
for the millions who drank tenebrous

black, contaminated raindrops to
stop the burning in their bodies.

Blood, diluted of cells,
gushing in the streets; hair instantly

falling, fire down to bone,
no morphine, no hospital standing.

I forced myself to listen to the
chemical tragedy to the end.

I was born two years later,
the world still reeling in whispers.

There are tulips on my table,
where are their tears?

Small birds singing in the
hedgerow, where are their tears?

People shopping for
Christmas, where are their tears?

The soldier who
piloted the plane, what of him?

The creators, in alcoholic dread of its'
apocalyptic magnitude, what of them?

ACKNOWLEDGEMENTS

Those who have helped at the building site of this book are many. Held aloft by family, community and strangers whose faces comfort me with their humanity, We are forged and battered to our bones by words. This is a true story from Jacques Lusseyran's memoir "And There Was Light." He tells about his time in Auschwitz. One day, a man stood in the courtyard reciting poetry, as the Poles were going to the gas chambers. Emaciated and barely human, prisoners gathered one by one, to form a circle, as though the words were food at that brutal hour. Everyday, they assembled to feed on sound that came out of the dark to love them. I want to thank words that have appeared when I needed them most, especially for their honesty. Nothing else is radical enough to change you. I want to acknowledge how sounds are music; the fall of the acorn, the forlorn bleat of birth, gasp of death and the wind at the edge of the sea. To thank so many people who have appeared on my path with the right words, especially the ones who showed up for my children. I need volumes to thank all of you. So many angels, so many angels in my life.

Judith Adams lives in the pacific North west on Whidbey island. She has written a number of poetry books, Springing the Hill, Crossing the Line, I Wanna Die Nice and Easy and Love Letters Only. Recordings of her books and public readings are also available. Her work has been choreographed for dance performance on the East Coast. She has had poems published in England and in America and has had two children's books published by Wynstones Press in England. Judith has been selected for the Washington State Humanities Speaker's Bureau for 2017/18 .

A ROBIN PRESS BOOK

www.judithadamscustompoetry.com
PO Box 1303, Langley, WA 98260
Email: judithalison.adams@gmail.com

INDEX

BOOK DESIGN: Roosje Wiedijk
www.mindthatbird.us

Made in the USA
Charleston, SC
28 January 2017